Impressum
Verlag: BABADADA GmbH, Nedderfeld 112 , 22529 Hamburg
Geschäftsführer / Verlagsleitung: Harald Hof
Druck: Books on Demand GmbH, In de Tarpen 42, 22848 Norderstedt

Imprint
Publisher: BABADADA GmbH, Nedderfeld 112 , 22529 Hamburg, Germany
Managing Director / Publishing direction: Harald Hof
Print: Books on Demand GmbH, In de Tarpen 42, 22848 Norderstedt

classroom
کلاس روم

divide
ونڈ کرنٹ

186/2

board
بورڈ

school yard
اسکول جو اگن

teacher
استاد

paper
کاغذ

write
لکھ

pen
پین

desk
میز

pupil
شاگرد

ruler
فٹ پٹی

book
کتاب

satchel
....
بستو

pencil case
....
پینسل باکس

pencil
....
پینسل

pencil sharpener
....
پینسل شارپنر

rubber
....
ربڑ

drawing pad
....
ڈرائنگ پیڈ

drawing

ڈرائنگ

paintbrush

پینٹ برش

paint box

پینٹ باکس

scissors

قینچي

glue

گوند

exercise book

مشق کرٹ واري کاپي

homework

ہوم ورک

12

number

عدد

2+2

add

جوڑ کرٹ

5-2

subtract

کٹ کرٹ

2×2

multiply

ضرب کرٹ

calculate

حساب کرٹ

A

letter

خط

ABCDEFG
HIJKLMN
OPQRSTU
VWXYZ

alphabet

الفابيٹ

hello

word

لفظ

text

مضمون

read

پَڑھڻ

chalk

چاڪ

lesson

سبق

register

رجسٽر

exam

امتحان

certificate

سرٽيفيڪيٽ

school uniform

اسڪول يونيفارم

education

تعليم

encyclopedia

انسائيڪلوپيڊيا

university

يونيورسٽي

microscope

خوربيني

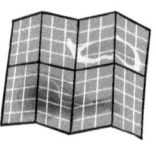

map

نقشو

waste-paper basket

ردي جي ٽوڪري

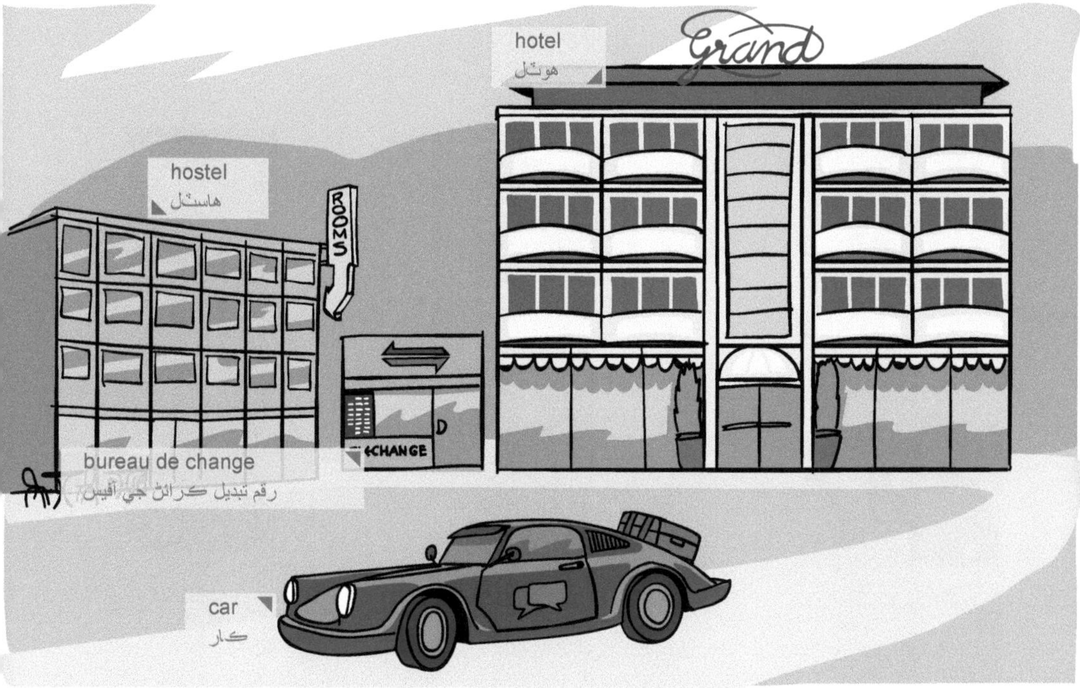

hotel
هوٽل
Grand
hostel
هاسٽل
ROOMS
bureau de change
رقم تبديل ڪرائڻ جي آفيس
CHANGE
car
ڪار

language
ٻولي

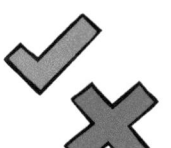

yes / no
ها يا نه

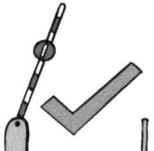

Okay
صحيح آهي

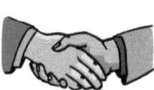

hello
هيلو

translator
مترجم

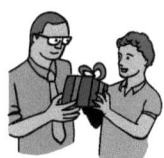

Thank you
مهرباني

how much is...?

هن جي قيمت گهڻي آهي.....؟

I do not understand

مون كي سمجھ ۾ نٿو اچي

problem

مسئلو

Good evening!

گڊ ايوننگ

Good morning!

صبح بخير

Good night!

شب خير

bye bye

الوداع

direction

طرف

luggage

سفري سامان

bag

بيگ

backpack

پويان ٻڌڻ وارو بيگ

guest

مهمان

room

كمرو

sleeping bag

بستر وارو بيگ

tent

خيمو

tourist information

سياحت بابت معلومات

beach

سمندر کنارو

credit card

کریډٹ کارډ

breakfast

ناشتو

lunch

لنچ

dinner

ډنر

ticket

ټکٹ

lift

لفٹ

stamp

مهر

border

سرحد

customs

ګاهک

embassy

سفارتخانو

visa

ویزا

passport

پاسپورٹ

transport

آمد و رفت

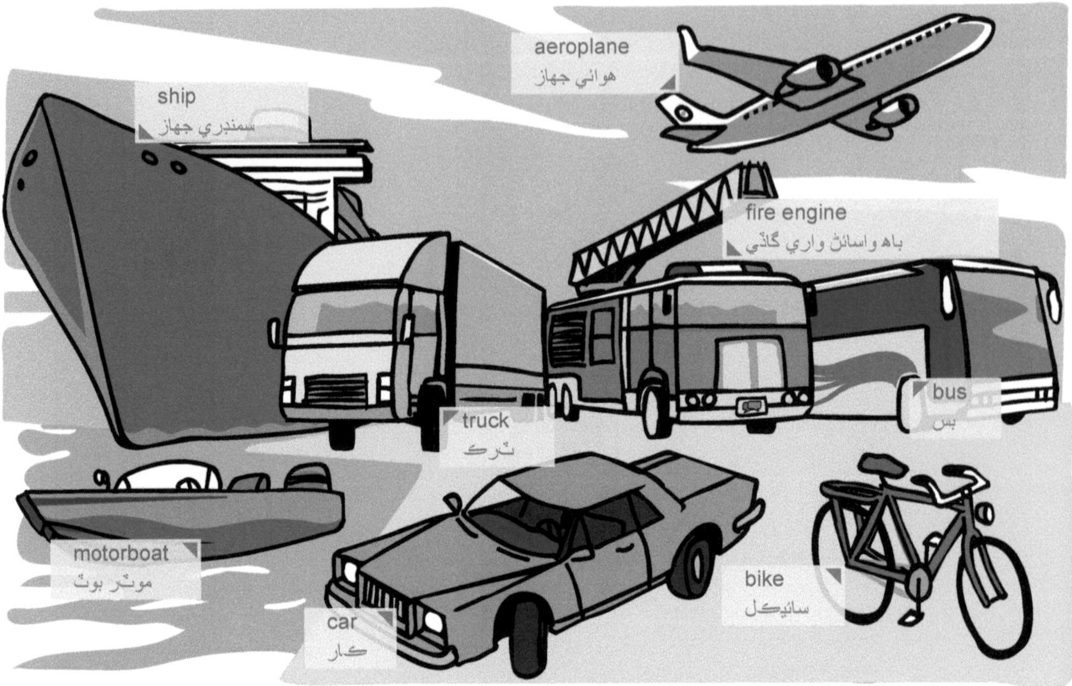
aeroplane
هوائي جهاز
ship
سمندري جهاز
fire engine
باھ وسائڻ واري گاڏي
bus
بس
truck
ٽرڪ
motorboat
موٽر بوٽ
bike
سائيڪل
car
ڪار

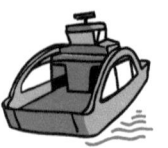

ferry

فيري

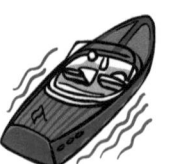

boat

بيڙي

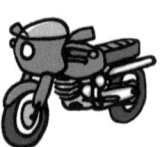

motorbike

موٽر سائيڪل

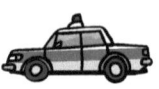

police car

پوليس ڪار

racing car

ريسنگ ڪار

rental car

رينٽل ڪار

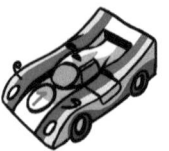

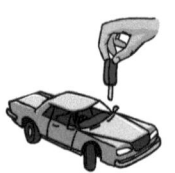

car sharing

چشنیرنگ کار

breakdown truck

چکڻ وارو ٽرڪ

refuse truck

ڪچري واري ٽرڪ

motor

ڪار

fuel

فيول

petrol station

پيٽرول اسٽيشن

traffic sign

ٽريفڪ جا نشان

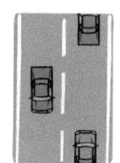

traffic

ٽريفڪ

traffic jam

ٽريفڪ جام

car park

ڪار پارڪ

train station

ٽرين اسٽيشن

tracks

پٽڙيون

train

ٽرين

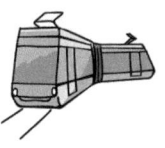

tram

ٽرام

carriage

ويگن

helicopter

هيليڪاپٽر

airport

ايئرپورٽ

tower

ٽاور

passenger

مسافر

container

ڪنٽينر

carton

ڊِٻو

cart

ريڙهي

basket

ٽوڪري

take off / land

اڏرڻ / زمين تي لهڻ

city

شهر

village

ڳوٺ

city centre

شهر جو مرڪز

house

گهر

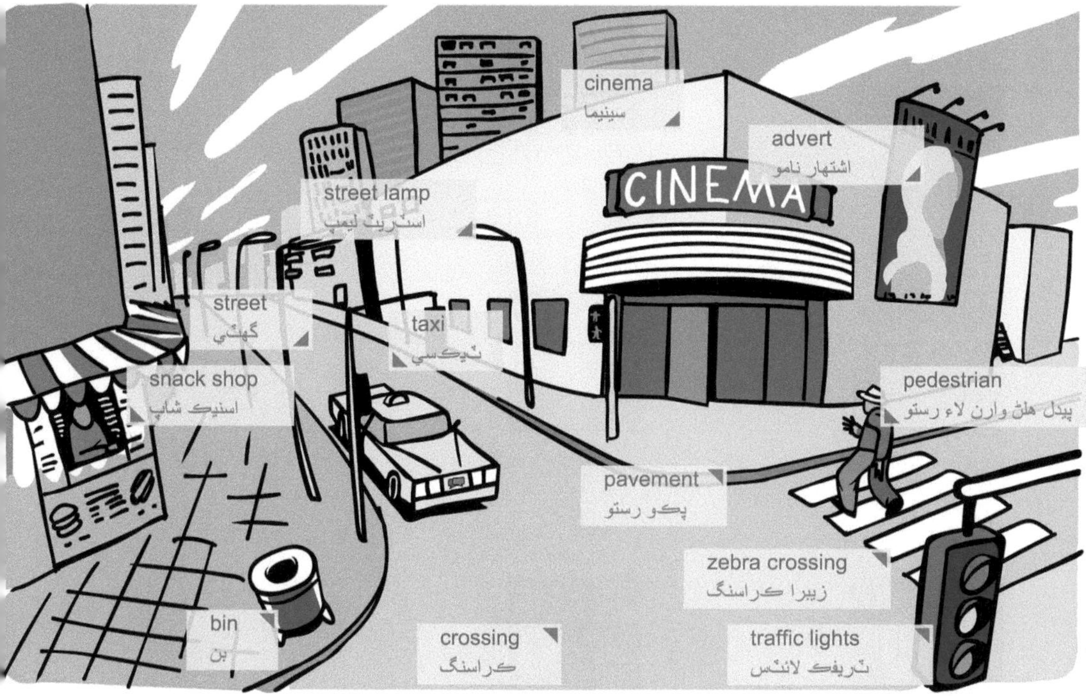
cinema
سینیما
advert
اشتهار نامو
CINEMA
street lamp
اسٽريٽ ليمپ
street
گهٽي
taxi
ٽيڪسي
snack shop
اسنيڪ شاپ
pedestrian
پيدل هلڻ وارن لاء رستو
pavement
پڪو رستو
zebra crossing
زيبرا ڪراسنگ
bin
بن
crossing
ڪراسنگ
traffic lights
ٽريفڪ لائٽس

hut
جهوپڙي

flat
فليٽ

train station
ٽرين اسٽيشن

town hall
ٽائون هال

MUSEUM
museum
عجائب گهر

school
اسڪول

university

يونيورسٽي

bank

بينڪ

hospital

اسپتال

hotel

هوٽل

pharmacy

فارميسي

office

آفس

book shop

ڪتابن جي ڪتاب

shop

دڪان

florist's

گلن جي دڪان

supermarket

سپر مارڪيٽ

market

مارڪيٽ

department store

ڊپارٽمينٽ اسٽور

fishmonger's

مڇي جي دڪان

shopping centre

شاپنگ سينٽر

harbour

بندرگاھ

park

پارک

bench

بینچ

bridge

پل

stairs

ڈاکٹ

underground

زیر زمین میٹرو

tunnel

سرنگ

bus stop

بس اسٹاپ

bar

شراب خانو

restaurant

روسٹورینٹ

postbox

پوسٹ باکس

street sign

اسٹریٹ سائن

parking meter

پارکنگ میٹر

zoo

چڑیا گھر

swimming pool

سوئمنگ پول

mosque

مسجد

farm

فارم

pollution

آلودگي

graveyard

قبرستان

church

چرچ

playground

راند جو ميدان

temple

مندر

landscape

زميني منظر

signpost
سائن بورڊ

way
رستو

meadow
ساوڪ واري زمين

stone
پٿر

hiker
پيادل هلڻ وارو هانيڪر

tree
وڻ

river
دريا

grass
چھر

flower
گل

valley

وادي

hill

جبل

lake

ڍنڊ

forest

ٻيلو

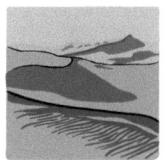

desert

ريگستان

volcano

آتش فشان

castle

قلعو

rainbow

اندلٺ

mushroom

کِيني

palm tree

کھجي جو وڻ

mosquito

مڇر

fly

مک

ant

ڪِولي

bee

ماکي جي مک

spider

مکڙي

beetle

ٹنڈڈ

frog

ڈیڈر

squirrel

نورینڑو

hedgehog

چاهو

hare

خرگوش

owl

چپرو

bird

پکي

swan

بدک

boar

سوئر

deer

هرڻ

moose

أمريكي هرڻ جو قسم

dam

ڈيم

wind turbine

هوا سان هلڻ واروٽربائين

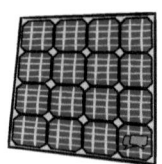

solar panel

سولر پينل

climate

آب و هوا

waiter
ويٽر

menu
کاڏي جي فهرست

chair
ڪرسي

soup
سوپ

pizza
پيزا

cutlery
ڇري ڪانٽا

tablecloth
ٽيبل جو ڪپڙو

starter
اسٽارٽر

main course
مين ڪورس

dessert
کاڏي کانپوء کائڻ وارو مٺو

drinks
مشروب

food
خوراڪ

bottle
بوتل

fast food

فاسٹ فوډ

street food

اسٹریټ فوډ

teapot

کتّلي

sugar bowl

شگر باؤل

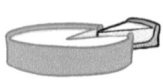

portion

تّکړو

espresso machine

ایسپریسو مشین

high chair

اونچي کرسي

bill

بل

tray

ټري

knife

چهري

fork

کانټو

spoon

چمچ

teaspoon

چائهن جر چمچو

serviette

سروینټي

glass

گلاس

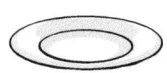

plate

پلیٹ

soup plate

سوپ پلیٹ

saucer

ساسر

sauce

چٹنی

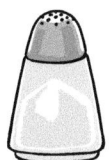

salt pot

لوڻ داني

pepper mill

مرچ پيسٽ وارو

vinegar

سرڪو

oil

ڪاڏو پچائڻ وارو تيل

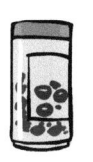

spices

مصالحو

ketchup

ڪيچ اپ

mustard

سرنهن

mayonnaise

مايونيز

supermarket
سپر مارڪيٽ

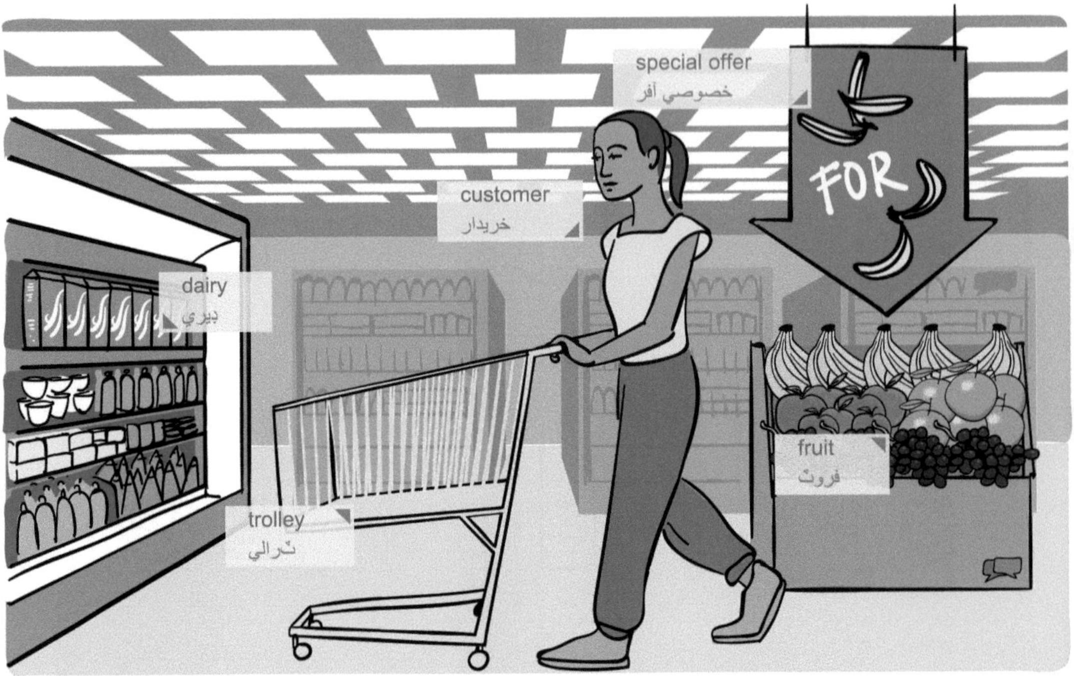

special offer
خصوصي آفر
FOR
customer
خريدار
dairy
ڊيري
fruit
فروٽ
trolley
ٽرالي

BUTCHERS

butcher´s

گوشت جي دڪان

BAKERY

baker´s

بيڪري

weigh

وزن ڪرڻ

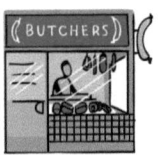

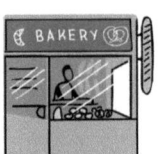

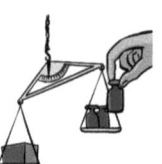

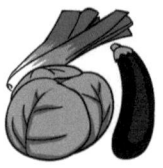

vegetables

سبزيون

meat

گوشت

frozen food

ڄميل کاڌو

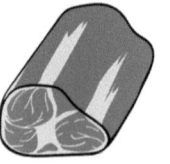

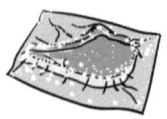

cold meat

سرد گوشت

tinned food

ڈبي ۾ بند کاڌو

washing powder

واشنگ پاؤڊر

sweets

مٺائي

household products

گھريلو سامان

cleaning products

صفائي کرڻ وارا پرابڪٽس

salesperson

سيلز پرسن

till

ڪيش رجسٽر

cashier

خزانچي

shopping list

خريداري جي فهرست

opening hours

اوقاتِ ڪار

wallet

پرس

credit card

ڪريڊٽ ڪارڊ

bag

بيگ

plastic bag

پلاسٽڪ بيگ

water

پاني

juice

جوس

milk

کیر

coke

کوک

wine

وائن

beer

بيئر

alcohol

الکوهل

cocoa

کوکو

tea

چاني

coffee

کافي

espresso

ايسپريسو

cappuccino

کپيوچينو

banana

کیلو

apple

صوف

orange

مالٹو

melon

خربوزو

lemon

لیمون

carrot

گجر

garlic

ٹھوم

bamboo

بانس

onion

بصر

mushroom

کٹیی

nuts

اخروٹ، بادام

noodles

نودلز

spaghetti

اسپيگټي

rice

چانور

salad

سلاد

chips

چپس

fried potatoes

تريل پټاټا

pizza

پيزا

hamburger

هيم برګر

sandwich

سينډوچ

cutlet

ګوشت جو نٽکرو

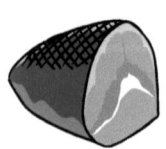

ham

سور جي ران جو ګوشت

salami

خشڪ ګوشت

sausage

ساسيج

chicken

مرغي

roast

روسټ

fish

مڇي

porridge oats

جو جو دليا

muesli

ميوزلي

cornflakes

كارن فليكس

flour

اٽو

croissant

كرؤئسنٽ

bread roll

بريڊ رول

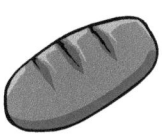

bread

بريڊ

toast

ٽوسٽ

biscuits

بسكٽ

butter

مکڻا

curd

دهي

cake

كيك

egg

انڊا

fried egg

فرائي ٿيل انڊو

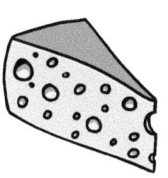

cheese

پنير

ice cream

آئس كريم

sugar

كنڈ

honey

ماكي

jam

مربو

chocolate spread

چاكليٹ اسپريڈ

curry

ڀاجي

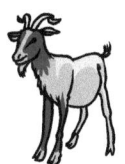

farm

فارم

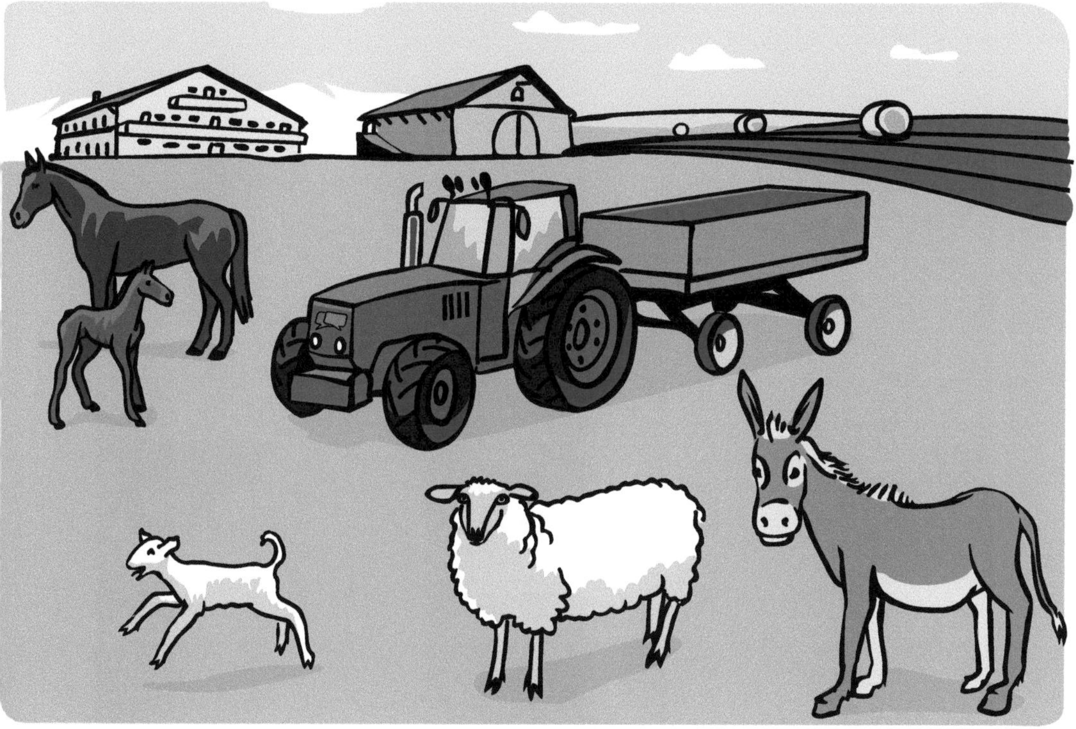

goat

ٻڪري

cow

ڳئون

calf

پاڏو

pig

سؤر

piglet

سؤر جو ٻچو

bull

ڍڳو

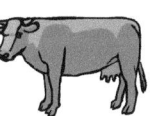

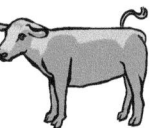

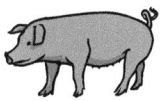

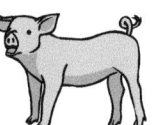

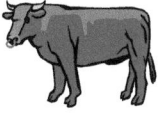

goose

هنس

duck

بدڪ

chick

چوزا

hen

مرغي

cock

مرغو

rat

ڪونو

cat

ٻلي

mouse

ڪونو

ox

ڳانڊ

dog

ڪتو

doghouse

ڪتي جو گهر

garden hose

گاردن هوز

watering can

پاڻي جو ڪين

scythe

ڏاٽو

plough

هر

28

sickle

ڏاٽو

hoe

رنبو

pitchfork

ڏانداري

axe

کھاڙو

wheelbarrow

هڪ سان هلائڻ واري ريڙهي

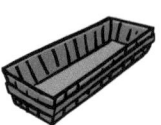

trough

حوض

milk can

کير جو ڏٻو

sack

ڳوٿ

fence

لوڙهو

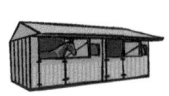

stable

اصطبل

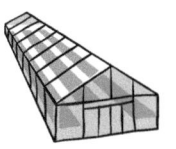

greenhouse

گرين هائوس

soil

مٽي

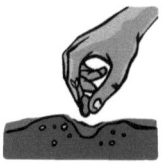

seed

ٻج

fertilizer

کھاد

combine harvester

ڪمبائنڊ هارويسٽر

harvest

فصل كــٹن

harvest

فصل كــٹن

yams

هك قسم جي تركاري

wheat

كـڻك

soy

سويا

potato

پٽاٽو

corn

مڪائي

rapeseed

توري جو ٻج

fruit tree

ميون جو وڻ

cassava

كساوا

cereals

اناج

house

گهر

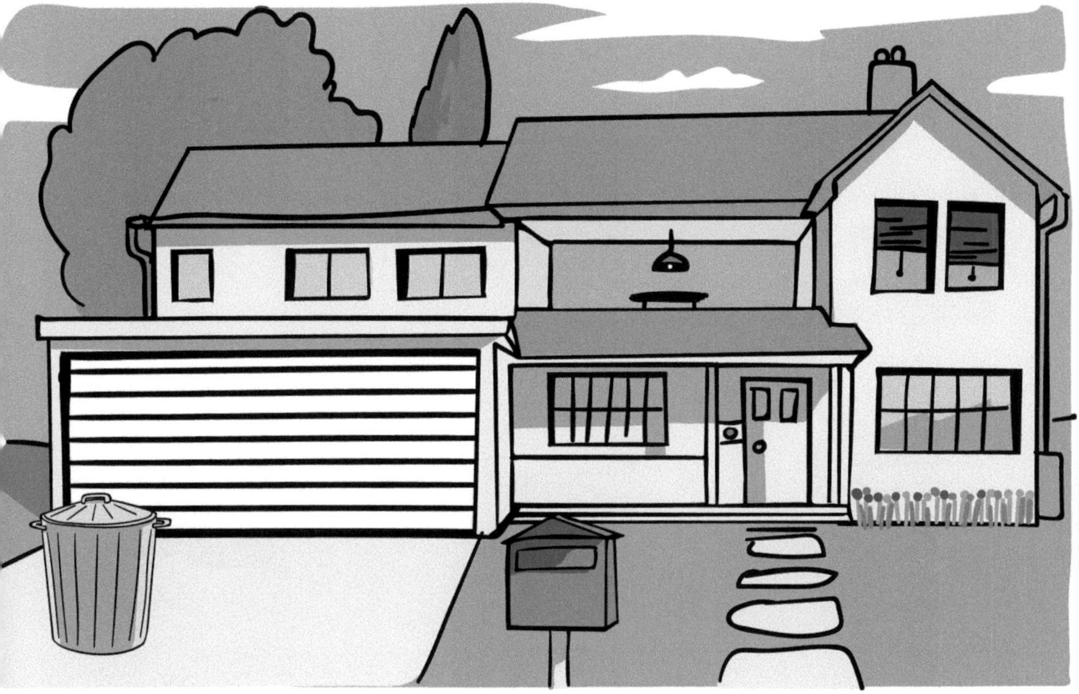

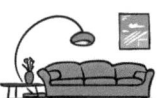

living room

لوونگ روم

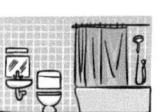

bathroom

غسل خانو

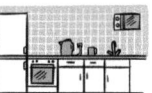

kitchen

باورچي خانو

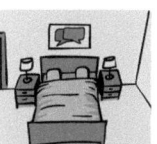

bedroom

بيڊروم

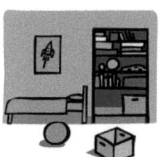

child's room

ٻارن جو ڪمرو

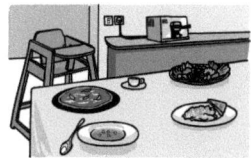

dining room

ڊائننگ روم

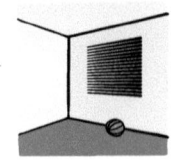

floor

فرش

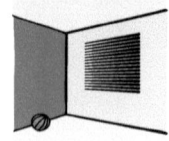

wall

ديوار

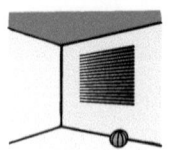

ceiling

چهت

cellar

تهخانو

sauna

ہاف وارو غسل

balcony

بالكوني

terrace

ٹيرس

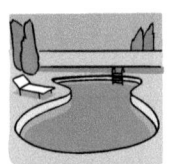

pool

تلاؤ

lawn mower

گاه كتڼ واري مشين

sheet

چادر

bedspread

چادر

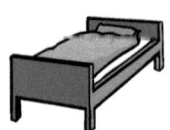

bed

بيډ

broom

جهاړو

bucket

بالټي

switch

سوټچ

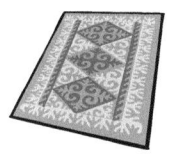

living room
لوونگ روم

carpet

قالين

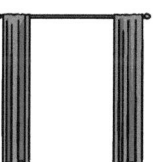

curtain

پردو

table

ميز

chair

ڪرسي

rocking chair

لڏڻ واري ڪرسي

armchair

آرام ڪرسي

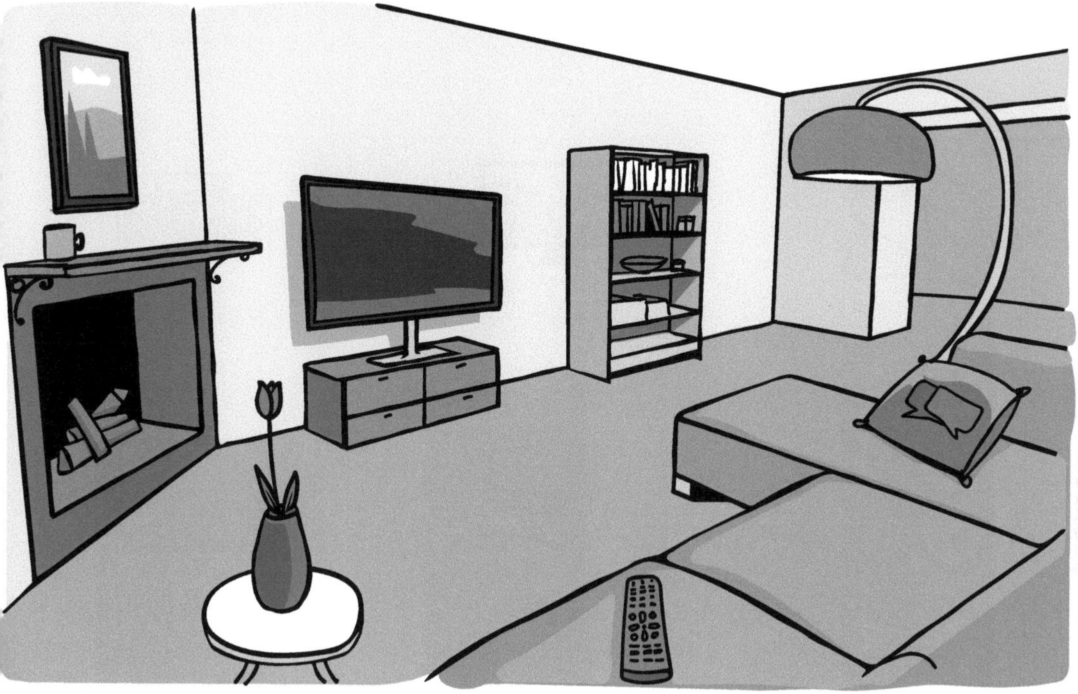

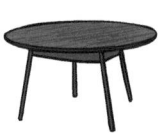

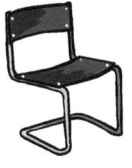

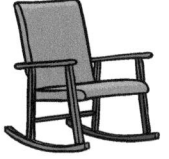

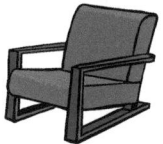

book

كتاب

blanket

كمبل

decoration

آرائش

firewood

ہارٹھ واريون كانئيون

film

فلم

hi-fi equipment

ھائی فائی

key

چابی

newspaper

اخبار

painting

پینٹنگ

poster

پوسٹر

radio

ریڈیو

notepad

نوٹ بك

hoover

ویكیوم كلینر

cactus

ٹوھر جو پوٹو

candle

میٹ بتی

kitchen

باورچي خانو

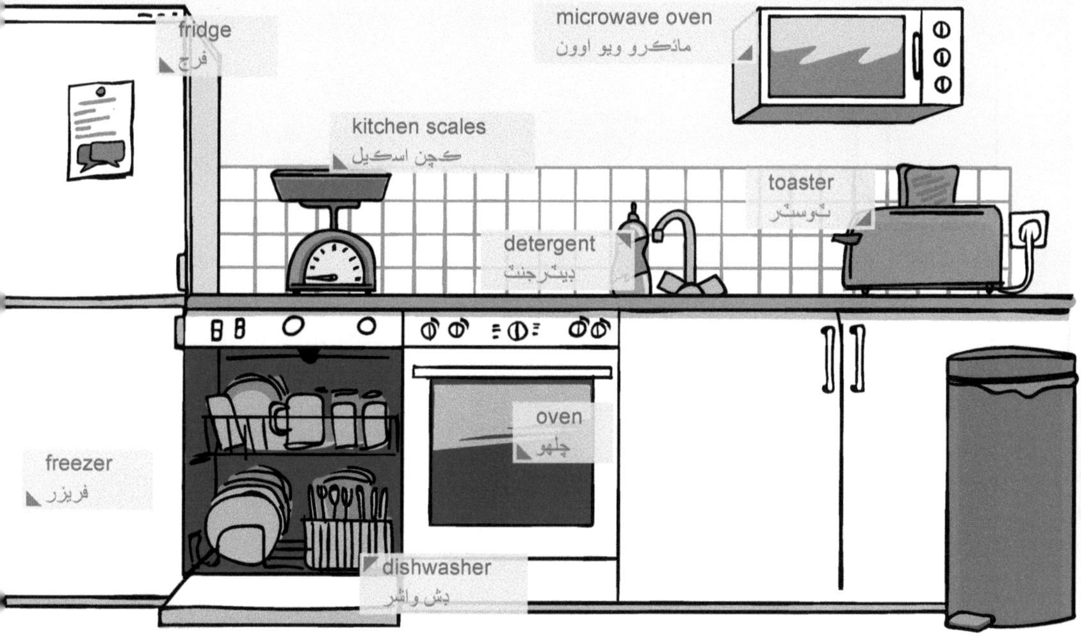
fridge
فرج
microwave oven
مائڪرو ويو اوون
kitchen scales
ڪچن اسڪيل
toaster
ٽوسٽر
detergent
ڊيٽرجنٽ
oven
چلهو
freezer
فريزر
dishwasher
ڊش واشر

cooker

ڪُڪر

pot

ٿانوَ

cast-iron pot

ڪاسٽ آئرن جا ٿانو

wok / kadai

ڪڙهائي

pan

ترڙ وارو ٿانو

kettle

ڪيٽلي

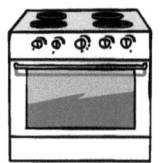

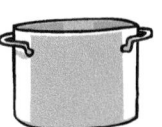

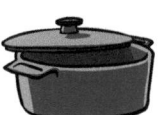

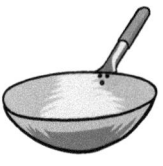

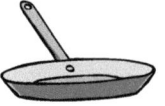

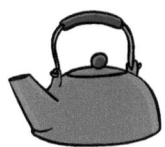

steamer

استيمر

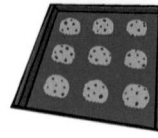

baking tray

بيكنگ ټري

crockery

کراکري

mug

مگ

bowl

پيالو

chopsticks

چاپ اسټکس

ladle

ډوئي

spatula

نفڅي

whisk

سبزي مكسر

strainer

چهاڼي

sieve

چهاڼي

grater

کدو کش وارو اوزار

mortar

اکري

barbecue

بار بي كيو

open fire

کليل باه

chopping board

سبزي ڪٽڻ وارو بورڊ

rolling pin

ويلڻ

corkscrew

ڪارڪ اسڪريو

can

ڪين

can opener

ڪين اوپنر

pot holder

ٽانوَ پڪڙڻ وارو ڪپڙو

sink

سنڪ

brush

برش

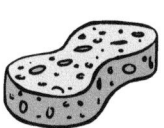

sponge

اسفنج

blender

بليندر

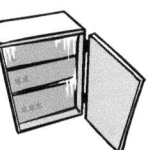

deep freezer

ڊيپ فريزر

baby bottle

بار جي بوتل

tap

نل

heating
هيٹنگ

shower
شاور

towel
ٹوال

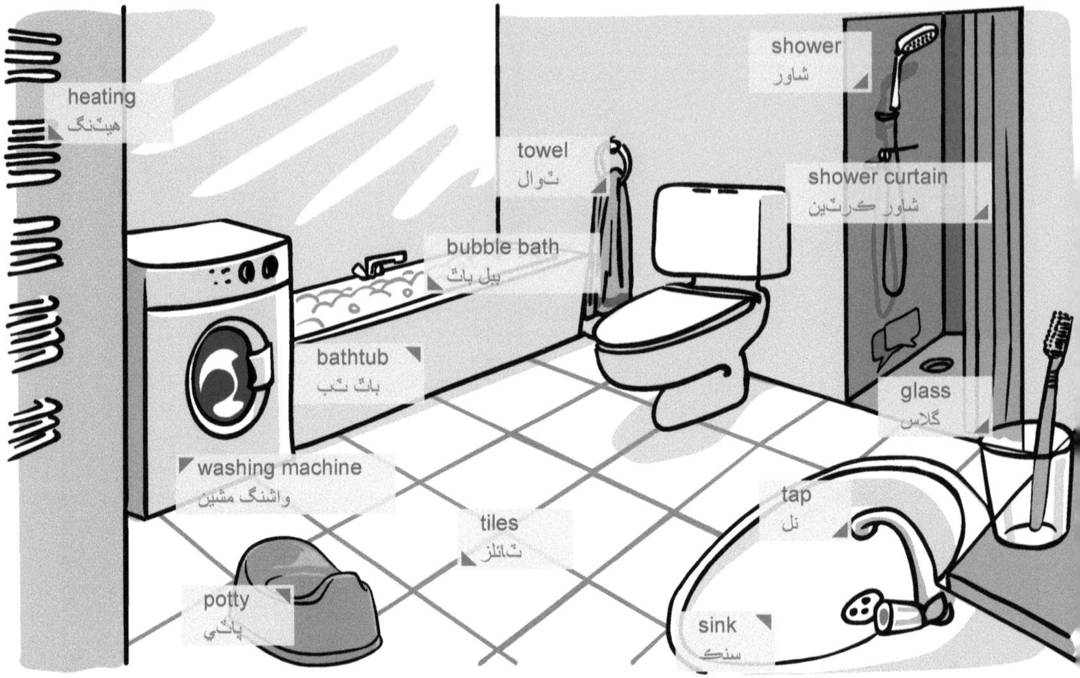

shower curtain
شاور کرٹين

bubble bath
ببل باٹ

bathtub
باٹ ٹب

glass
گلاس

washing machine
واشنگ مشين

tap
نل

tiles
ٹائلز

potty
پاٹي

sink
سنک

toilet
....
ٹائلٹ

squat toilet
....
اوکڑو ويهڻ وارو ٹوائلٹ

bidet
....
ٹرم گاه ٹونڻ وارو ٹب

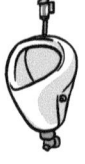

urinal
....
پيشاب گاه

toilet paper
....
ٹائلٹ پيپر

toilet brush
....
ٹائلٹ برش

toothbrush

ٹوتھ برش

toothpaste

ٹوتھ پیسٹ

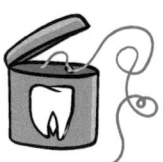

dental floss

ڈینٹل فلاس

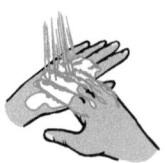

wash

دَھونڑ

handheld shower

ہینڈ شاور

douche

شاور

basin

بیسِن

back brush

بیک برش

soap

صابن

shower gel

شاور جیل

shampoo

شیمپو

flannel

فلالین

drain

ڈرین

cream

کریم

deodorant

ڈیوڈورنٹ

mirror

آئينو

hand mirror

هټ م پکړئ وارو آئينو

razor

ريزر

shaving foam

شيونگ فوم

aftershave

آفتر شيو

comb

ږمنځ

brush

برش

hair dryer

هيئر درائير

hairspray

هيئر اسپري

makeup

ميک اپ

lipstick

سرخي

nail varnish

نيل وارنش

cotton wool

کپه

nail scissors

نيل سيزر

perfume

پرفيوم

washbag

واش بیگ

stool

اسٹول

weighing scale

وزن کرٹ واري مشین

bathrobe

باتھ روب

rubber gloves

ربڑ جا دستانا

tampon

ٹیمپون

sanitary towel

صفائي وارو ٹاول

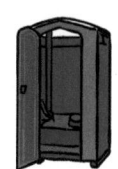

chemical toilet

کیمیائي ٹوائلٹ

child's room

ٻارن جو ڪمرو

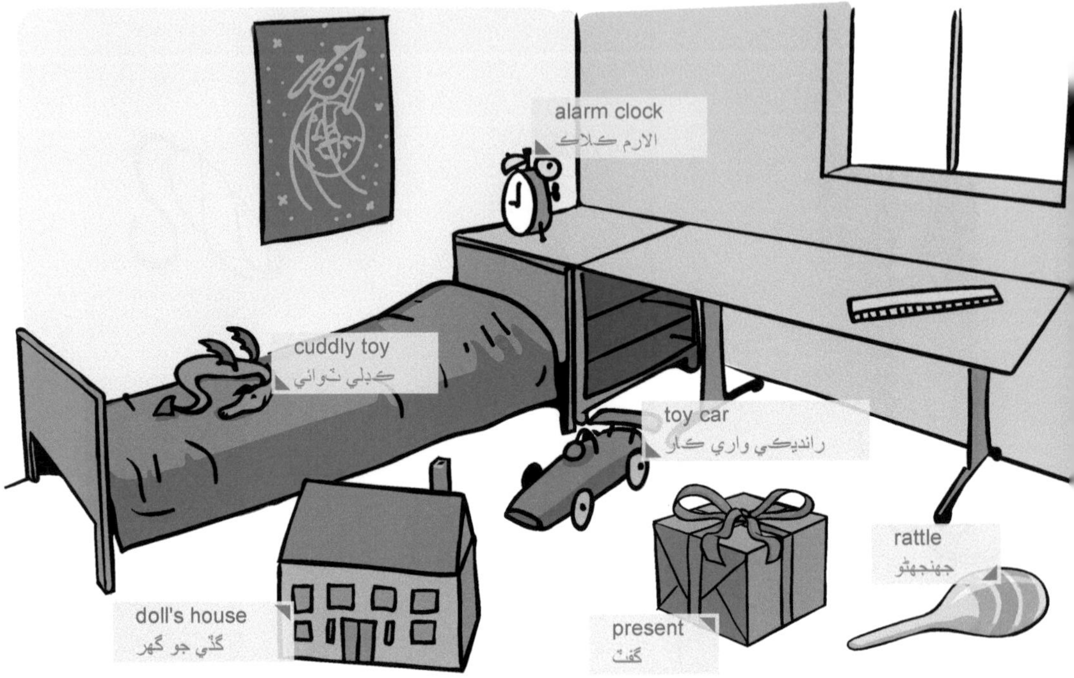

alarm clock
الارم ڪلاڪ
cuddly toy
ڪڊلي ٽوائي
toy car
رانديڪي واري ڪار
rattle
جهنجهڻو
doll's house
گڏي جو گهر
present
گفٽ

balloon

ڦوڪڻو

bed

بيڊ

pram

ٻار جي ڳاڏي

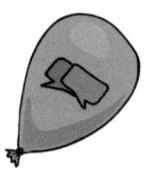

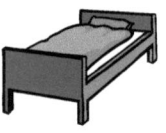

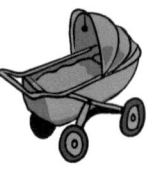

deck of cards

ڊيڪ آف ڪارڊز

jigsaw

جگسا

SUPER MEGA

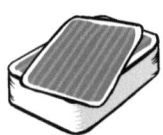

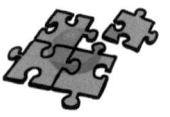

comic

ڪامڪ

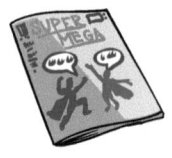

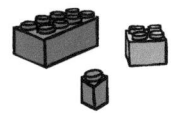

lego bricks

ليگوبرڪس

building blocks

رانديڪن وارا بلاڪس

action figure

ايڪشن فگر

babygrow

بيبي گرو

frisbee

فرسبي

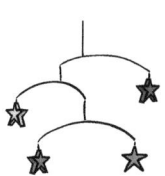

mobile

رانديڪي واري موبائل

board game

بورڊ گيم

dice

چهڪو

model train set

ماڊل ٽرين سيٽ

dummy

بارن جي چوسڻ واري نپل

party

پارٽي

picture book

تصوير واري ڪتاب

ball

بال

doll

گڏي

play

کيڏڻ

sandpit

سينڊ پٽ

swing

جهولا

toys

رانديڪا

video game console

وڊيو گيم ڪنسول

tricycle

ٽن ڦيٿن واري سائيڪل

teddy bear

ٽيڊي بيئر

wardrobe

ڪپڙن جي الماري

clothing

لباس

socks

جرابا

stockings

اسٽاڪنگز

tights

ٽائيٽس

scarf
اسكارف

umbrella
چَھتي

t-shirt
ٽي شرٽ

belt
بيلٽ

boots
بوٽ

slippers
چپل

trainers
جاگر شوز

sandals
سينڊل

shoes
جوتا

rubber boots
ربڙ جا بوٽ

underpants
انڊرپينٽس

bra
بريزر

vest
واسڪٽ

body

جسم

trousers

پتلون

jeans

جينز پينٹ

skirt

اسکرٹ

blouse

چولو

shirt

قميض

pullover

جرسي

hoodie

ہوڈي

blazer

بليزر

jacket

جيکٹ

coat

کوٹ

raincoat

بارش م پائٹ وارو کوٹ

costume

پوشاک

dress

لباس

wedding dress

شادي جولباس

suit

سوٽ

nightgown

نائٽ گائون

pyjamas

پاجامو

sari

ساڙي

headscarf

مٿي تي بڌل وارو اسڪارف

turban

پڳڙي

burqa

برقعو

kaftan

ڪفتان

abaya

عبايو

swimsuit

تيراڪي جو لباس

trunks

چڏي

shorts

نيڪر

tracksuit

ٽريڪ سوٽ

apron

اپرن

gloves

دستانا

button

بٹن

glasses

چشمو

bracelet

بریسلیٹ

necklace

هار

ring

منڈی

earring

والیون

cap

ٹوپي

coat hanger

کوٹ ہینگر

hat

ٹوپي

tie

ٹائي

zip

زپ

helmet

ہیلمٹ

braces

بریسز

school uniform

اسکول یونیفارم

uniform

وردي

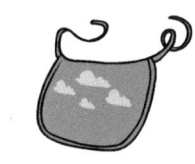

bib

ٻارن لاءِ ڳلي ۾ ٻڌڻ وارو ڪپڙو

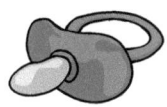

dummy

ٻارن جي چوسڻ واري نپل

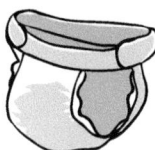

nappy

ڪڇو

office

آفس

server
سرور
filing cabinet
فائلن جي الماري
printer
پرنٽر
paper
ڪاغذ
monitor
مانيٽر
mouse
ماؤس
desk
ميز
folder
فولڊر
keyboard
ڪي بورڊ
waste-paper basket
ردي جي ٽوڪري
computer
ڪمپيوٽر
chair
ڪافي مگ

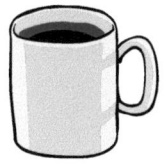

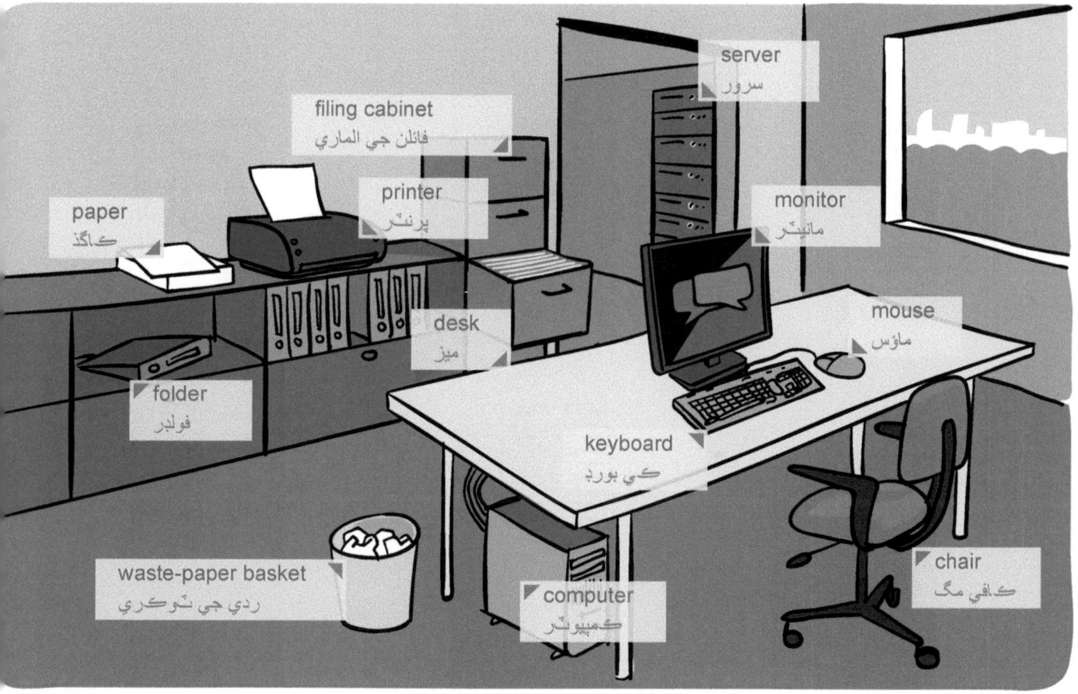

coffee mug

ڪافي مگ

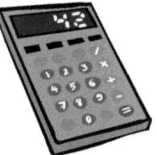

calculator

ڪيلڪيوليٽر

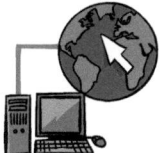

internet

انٽرنيٽ

laptop

لیپ ٹاپ

letter

خط

message

پیغام

mobile

موبائل

network

نیٹ ورک

photocopier

فوٹو کاپی کرٹ واری مشین

software

سافٹ ویئر

telephone

ٹیلی فون

plug socket

پلگ ساکٹ

fax machine

فیکس مشین

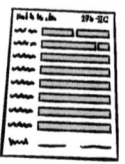

form

فارم

document

دستاویز

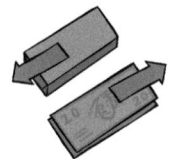

buy

خرید کرنٔ

pay

ادا کرنٔ

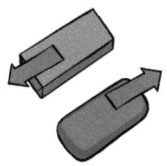

trade

صاف کرنٔ

money

پیسہ

dollar

ڈالر

euro

یورو

yen

یین

rouble

روبل

Swiss franc

سوئس فرانک

renminbi yuan

رینمینبی یوآن

rupee

روپیہ

cashpoint

کیش پوائنٹ

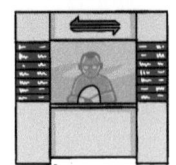

bureau de change

رقم تبديل كرائٹ جي آفيس

gold

سون

silver

چاندي

oil

خام تيل

energy

توانائي

price

قيمت

contract

معاهدو

tax

ٹيكس

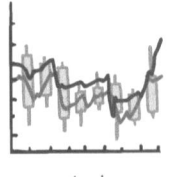

stock

ذخيرو

work

كم كرڻ

employee

ملازم

employer

آجر

factory

فيكٽري

shop

دڪان

occupations

پيشو

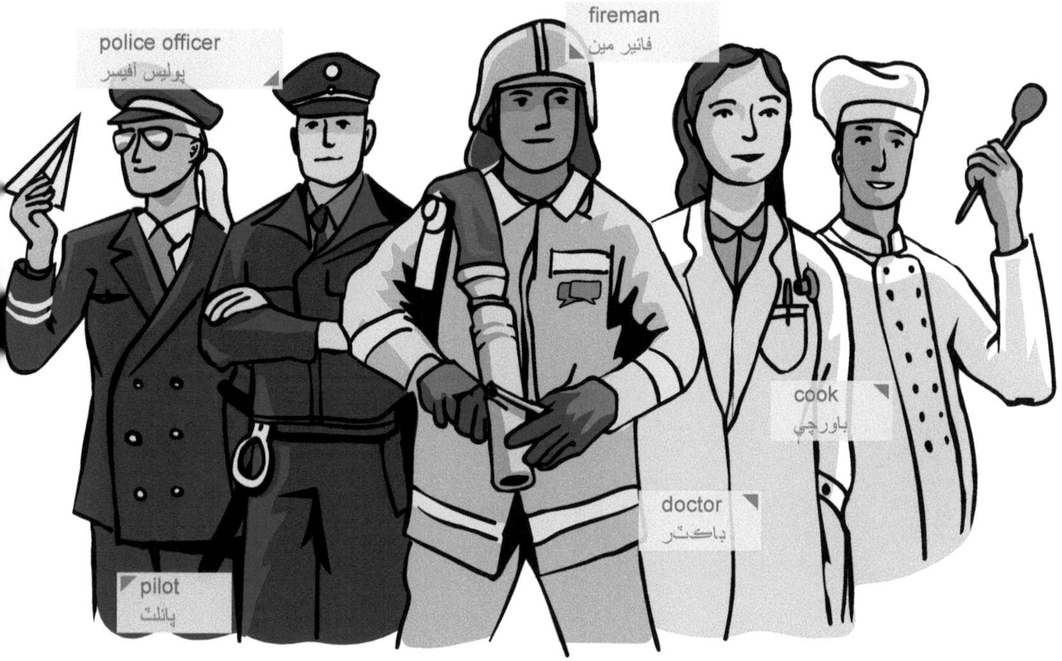
police officer
پولیس افیسر
fireman
فائیر مین
cook
باورچي
doctor
ډاکټر
pilot
پائلټ

gardener

مالي

carpenter

وايو

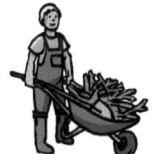

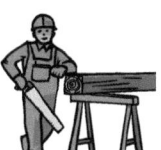

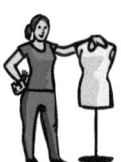

seamstress

درزن

judge

جج

chemist

کیمیسټ

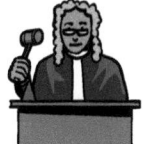

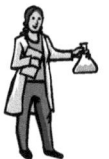

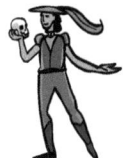

actor

اداکار

bus driver

بس ڊرائيور

taxi driver

ٽيڪسي ڊرائيور

fisherman

مڇي مارڻ وارو

cleaning lady

صفائي ڪرڻ واري ماني

roofer

ڇت ڄاهڻ وارو

waiter

ويٽر

hunter

شڪاري

painter

رنگ ساز

baker

نانوائي

electrician

اليڪٽريشن

builder

بلڊر

engineer

انجنيئر

butcher

ڪاسائي

plumber

پلمبر

postman

پوسٽ مين

soldier

سپاهي

architect

آركيٽيڪٽ

cashier

خزانچي

florist

گل کپائڻ وارو

hairdresser

نائي

conductor

ڪنڊيڪٽر

mechanic

مڪينڪ

captain

ڪپتان

dentist

ڊينٽسٽ

scientist

سائنسدان

rabbi

يهودي عالم

imam

امام

monk

راهب

clergyman

پادري

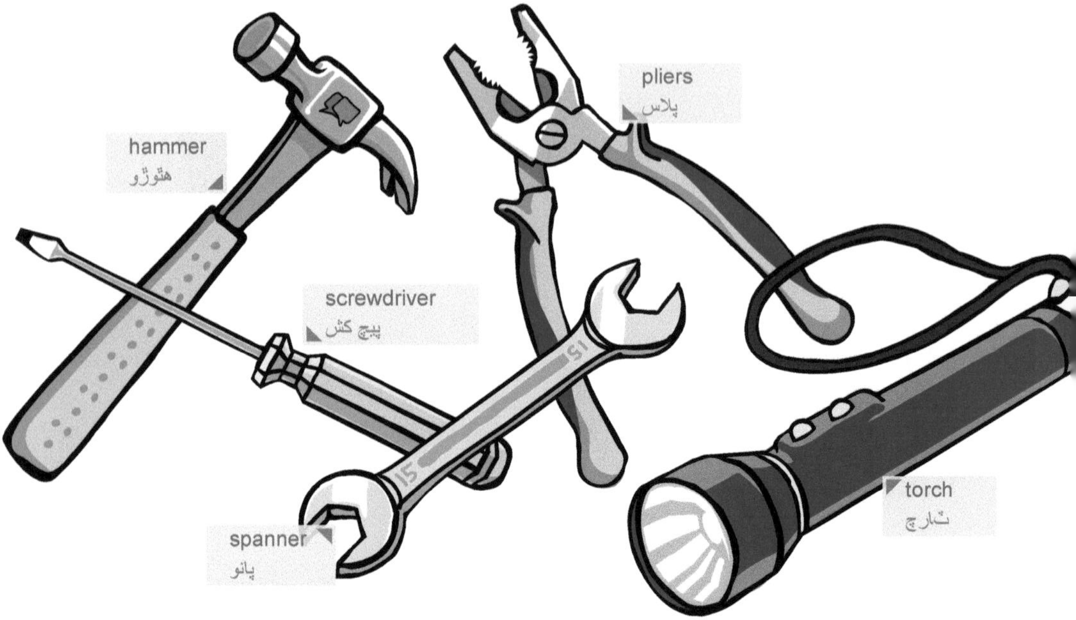

hammer
هتوړو

screwdriver
پیچ کش

pliers
پلاس

spanner
پانو

torch
ټارچ

digger

ایکسکویټر

toolbox

ټول باکس

ladder

ناکڼ

saw

آري

nails

کوکو

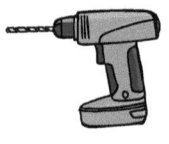

drill

برل

repair

مرمت ڪرڻ

shovel

بيلچو

Damn!

لعنت هجي!

dustpan

ڪچري دان

paint pot

پينٽ وارو ڊٻو

screws

پيچ

musical instruments

موسيقي جا اوزار

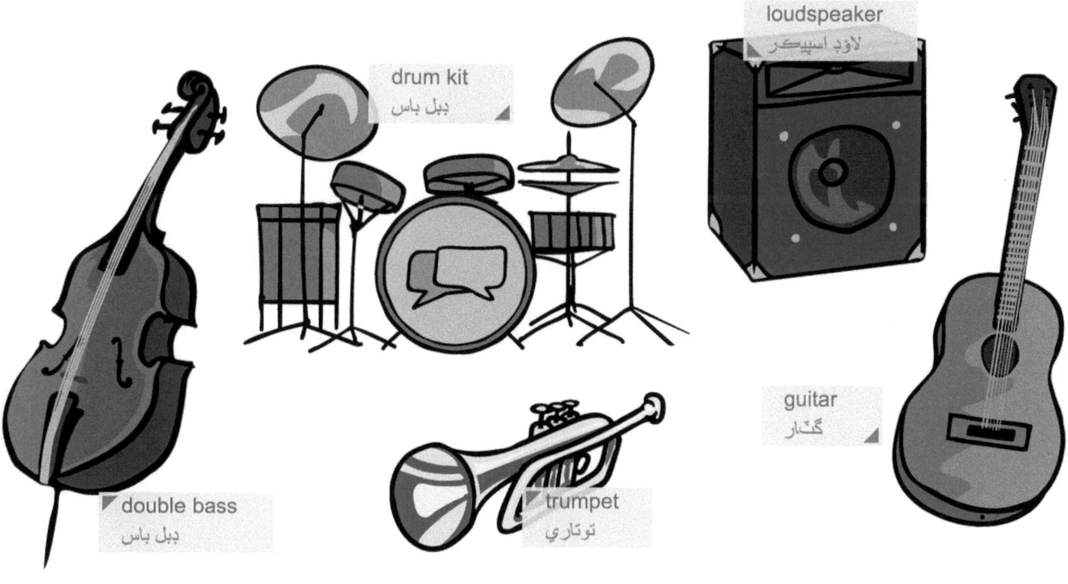

loudspeaker

لائوڊ اسپيڪر

drum kit

ڊبل باس

guitar

گٽار

double bass

ڊبل باس

trumpet

توتاري

piano

پيانو

violin

وائلن

bass

گٹار

timpani

ٹمپاني

drums

ڈرم

keyboard

كي بورڈ

saxophone

سيڪوفون

flute

بانسري

microphone

مائيكروفون

entrance
داخل ٿيڻ جو رستو ◄

tiger
چيتا

cage
پڃرو

zebra
زيبرا

animal feed
جانورن جي خوراڪ

panda
پانڊو

animals
....
جانور

elephant
....
هاٿي

kangaroo
....
ڪينگرو

rhino
....
گينڊو

gorilla
....
گوريلو

bear
....
رڇ

camel

اٹ

ostrich

شتر مرغ

lion

شینهن

monkey

بولڑو

flamingo

فلیمنگو

parrot

طوطو

polar bear

برفانی رچ

penguin

کبوتر

shark

شارک

peacock

مور

snake

نانگ

crocodile

واڱون

zookeeper

چڑیا گھر جو محافظ

seal

گوج مڇي

jaguar

چیتو

pony

ٹٹّون

leopard

چیتو

hippo

دریائی گھوڑو

giraffe

چِزراف

eagle

باز

boar

سوئر

fish

مچّھی

turtle

کمي

walrus

ساموندي گھوڑو

fox

لومڑي

gazelle

ھرڻ

American football
آمریکن فوتبال

cycling
سائکلنگ

tennis
ٹینس

basketball
باسکٹ بال

swimming
تیراکی

boxing
باکسنگ

ice hockey
آئس هاکی

football
فوٹبال

badminton
بیڈمنٹن

athletics
ایتهلیٹکس

handball
هینڈ بال

skiing
اسکیئنگ

polo
پولو

activities

سرگرميون

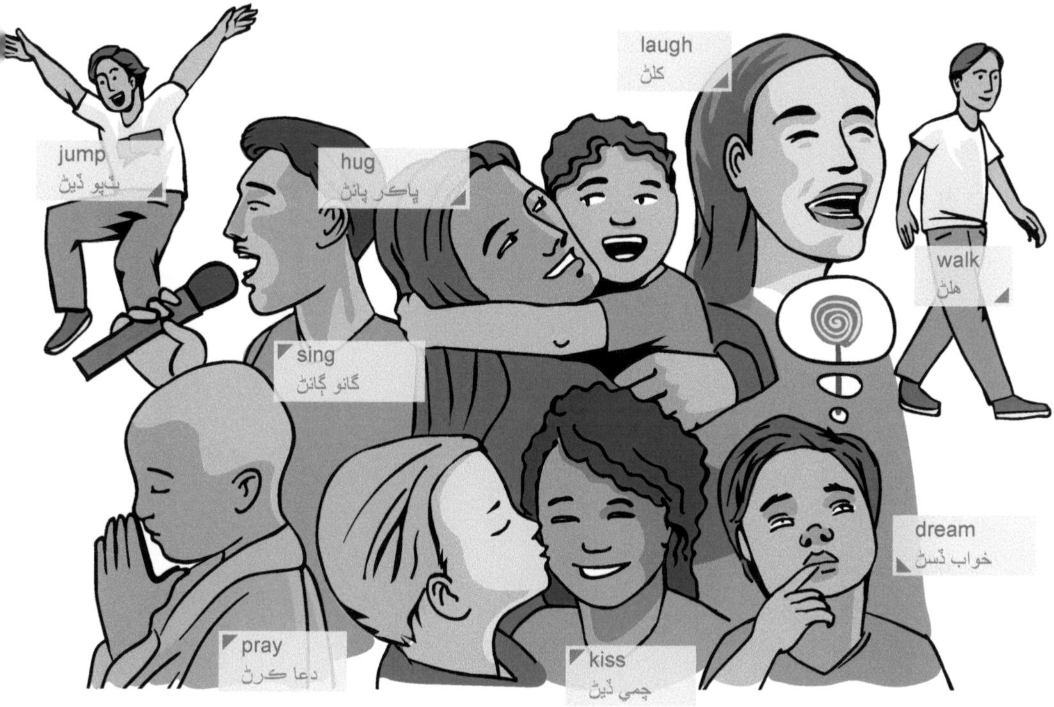

jump
ٽپو ڏيڻ
hug
ڀاڪر پائڻ
laugh
کلڻ
walk
هلڻ
sing
گانو ڳائڻ
dream
خواب ڏسڻ
pray
دعا ڪرڻ
kiss
چمي ڏيڻ

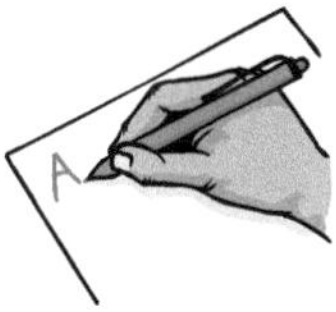

write

لکڻ

draw

تصوير ڪشي ڪرڻ

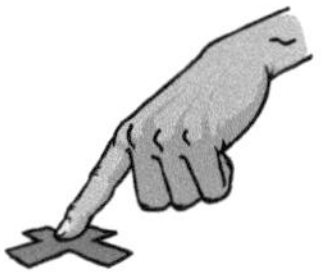

show

ڏيکارڻ

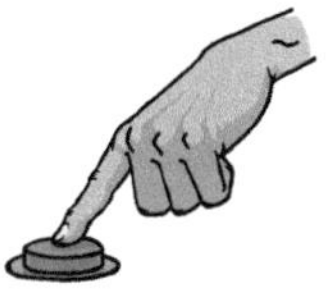

push

ڌڪو ڏيڻ

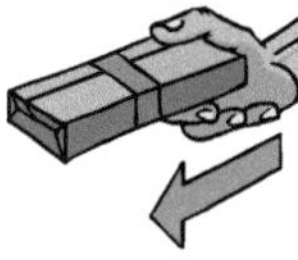

give

ڏيڻ

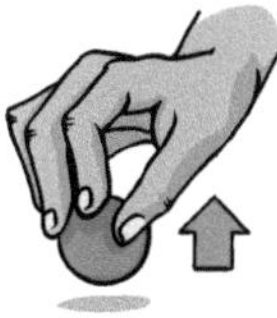

take

وٺڻ

have

 رکڻ

do

ڪرڻ

be

ٿيڻ

stand

بيھڻ

run

ڊوڙڻ

pull

ڇڪڻ

throw

اڇلائڻ

fall

ڪرڻ

lie

ڪروٽ ڀالھائڻ

wait

انتظار ڪرڻ

carry

کڻي وڃڻ

sit

ويھڻ

get dressed

تيار ٿيڻ

sleep

سمھڻ

wake up

جاڳڻ

look at

ٹَست

cry

رونٹ

stroke

ڈَک ھٹ

comb

کنگي کرٹ

talk

گالھائٹ

understand

سمجھٹ

ask

پُچٹ

listen

ہَتٹ

drink

پیئٹ

eat

کائٹ

tidy up

صاف کرٹ

love

پیار کرٹ

cook

پچائٹ

drive

گاڈي ھلائٹ

fly

اڑٹ

sail

بحري سفر كرڻ

calculate

حساب كرڻ

read

پڙهڻ

learn

سکڻ

work

كم كرڻ

marry

شادي كرڻ

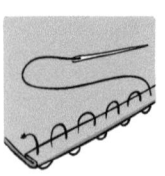

sew

سيئڻ

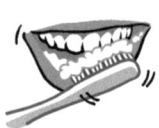

brush teeth

ڏندن كي برش كرڻ

kill

قتل كرڻ

smoke

سگريٽ پيئڻ

send

موكلڻ

grandmother
ڏاڏي يا ناني

grandfather
ڏاڏو يا نانو

father
پيُ

mother
ماءُ

baby
ٻار

daughter
ڌِيءَ

son
پُٽُ

guest
مهمان

aunt
چاچي

uncle
چاچو

brother
ڀاءُ

sister
ڀيڻ

forehead
پیشانی

eye
اک

shoulder
کلھو

finger
اگر

face
منھن

chin
کاٺي

hand
ھٿ

breast
چاتي

leg
ٽنگ

arm
بانھن

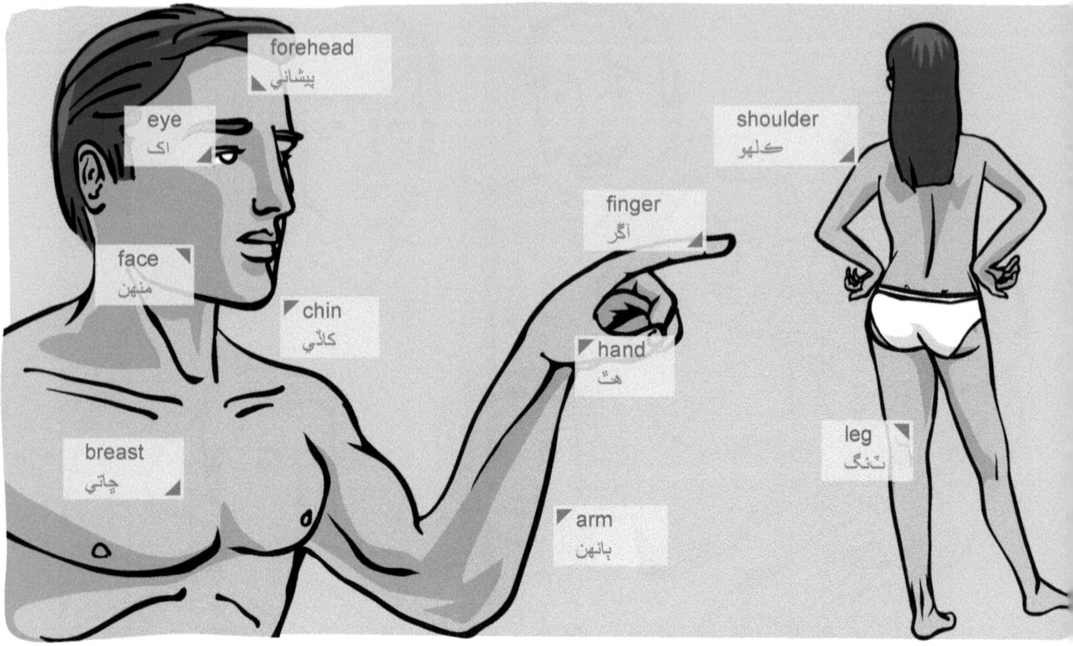

baby
....
ٻار

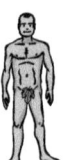

man
....
ماٺھون

woman
....
عورت

girl
....
چوکري

boy
....
چوکرو

head
....
مٿو

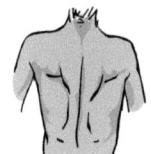

back

پٺي

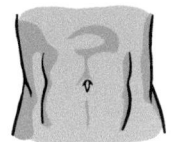

belly

پيٽ

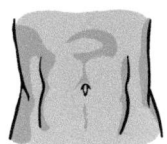

belly button

دن

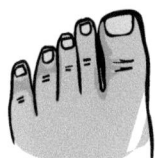

toe

پير جو آڱوٺو

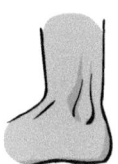

heel

کڙي

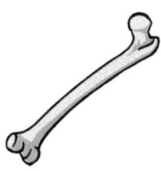

bone

هڏي

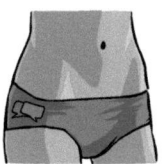

hip

ڦُندٽ

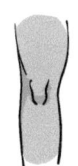

knee

گوڏو

elbow

ٺونٺ

nose

نڪ

bottom

هيٺيون حصو

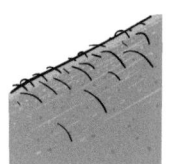

skin

کل

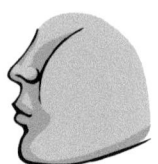

cheek

ڳل

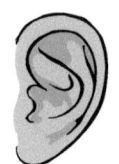

ear

ڪن

lip

چپ

body - جسم   69

mouth

وات

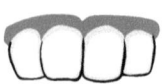

tooth

ڈند

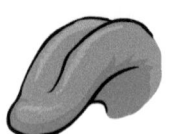

tongue

زبان

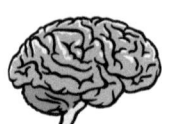

brain

دماغ

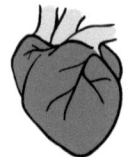

heart

دل

muscle

ٹورو

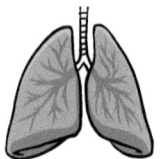

lung

پپھڑ

liver

جگر

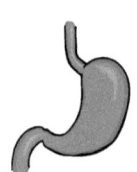

stomach

معدو

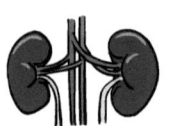

kidneys

گردا

sex

جماع کرن

condom

کندوم

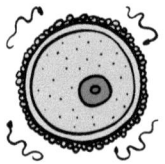

ovum

بیضہ

semen

منی

pregnancy

حمل

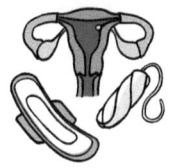

menstruation

حيض

vagina

ٻچيداني جي نالي

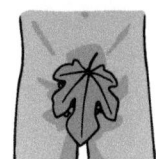

penis

مردانو مخصوص عضوو

eyebrow

پرون

hair

وار

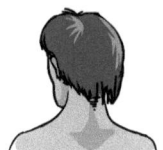

neck

ڳچي

hospital

اسپتال

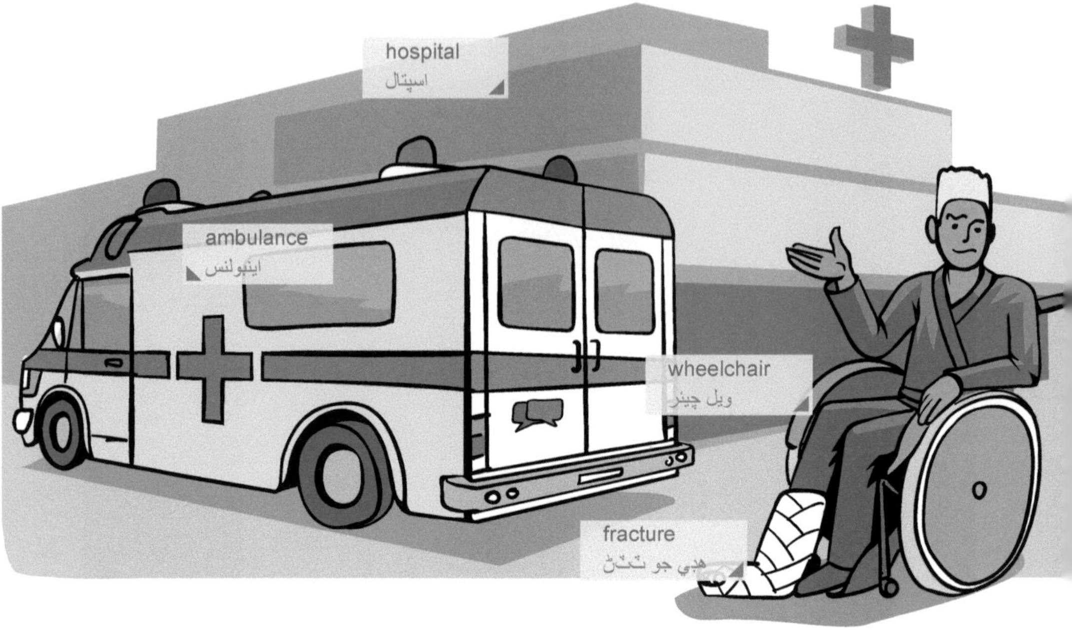

hospital
اسپتال
ambulance
اينبولنس
wheelchair
ويل چيئر
fracture
هڏي جو ٽٽڻ

doctor

ڊاڪٽر

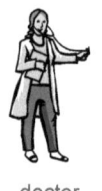

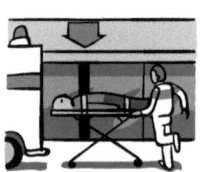

emergency room

هنگامي ڪمرو

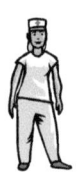

nurse

نرس

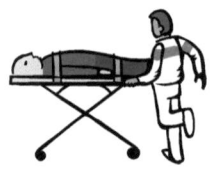

emergency

ايڪسري

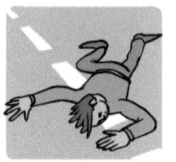

unconscious

بيهوش

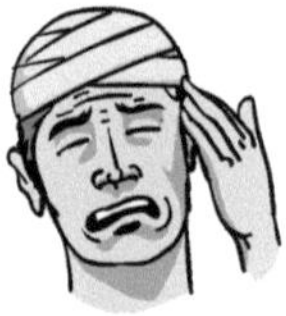

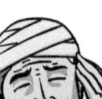

pain

سور

injury

زخم

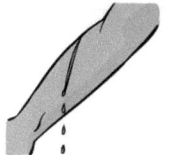

bleeding

رت وهڻ

heart attack

دل جو دورو

stroke

فالج

allergy

الرجي

cough

کنگھه

fever

بخار

flu

زڪام

diarrhoea

دست

headache

مٿي جو سور

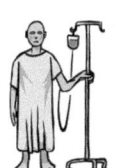

cancer

ڪينسر

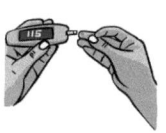

diabetes

ذيابيطس

surgeon

سرجن

scalpel

جراحي بليڊ

operation

آپريشن

CT

سي ٽي

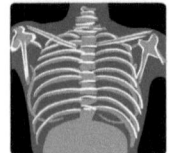

x-ray

ايڪسري

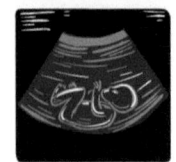

ultrasound

الٽراساؤنڊ

face mask

منهن جي ماسڪ

disease

بيماري

waiting room

انتظار ڪرڻ جو ڪمرو

crutch

بيساکِھي

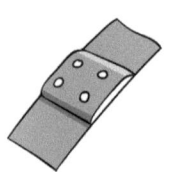

plaster

پالاسٽر

bandage

پٽي

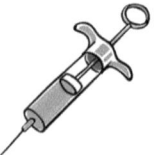

injection

انجيڪشن

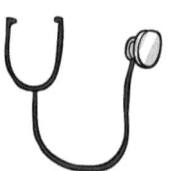

stethoscope

اسٽيٿوسڪوپ

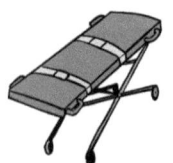

stretcher

اسٽريچر

clinical thermometer

ٿرماميٽر

birth

پيدائش

overweight

موٽاپو

hearing aid

ہٹرڈ واري ڈيوائس

disinfectant

جراثيم كش

infection

انفيكشن

virus

وائرس

HIV / AIDS

ايچ آئ وي / ايڈز

medicine

دوا

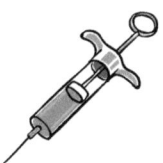

vaccination

ويكسينيشن

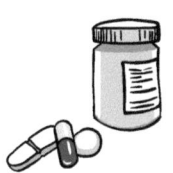

tablets

ٹكي

pill

گولي

emergency call

ہنگامي كال

blood pressure monitor

بلڈ پريشر مانيٹر

ill / healthy

بيمار / صحت

alarm

الارم

assault

جسماني حملو ڪرڻ

Help!

مدد

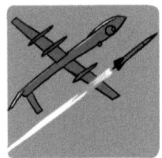

attack

حملو ڪرڻ

danger

خطره

emergency exit

هنگامي حالت ۾ نڪرڻ جو رستو

Fire!

باھ

fire extinguisher

باھ وسائڻ جو اوزار

accident

حادثو

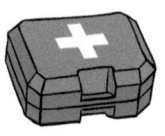

first-aid kit

ابتدائي طبي امداد

SOS

ايس او ايس

police

پوليس

Europe

یورپ

North America

اتر آمریکا

South America

ڈکڑ آمریکا

Africa

آفریقا

Asia

ایشیا

Australia

آسٹریلیا

Atlantic

اٹلانٹک

Pacific

پیسفک

Indian Ocean

بحر ہند

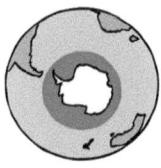

Antarctic Ocean

انٹارکٹک سمندر

Arctic Ocean

آرکٹک سمندر

North Pole

اتر قطب

South Pole

ذکٹ قطب

Antarctica

انٹارکٹیکا

Earth

زمین

land

زمین

sea

سمندر

island

جزیرو

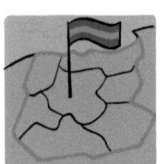

nation

قوم

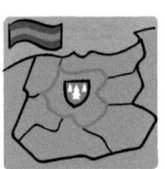

state

ریاست

clock face

گهڙي جو سامهون حصو

hour hand

ڪلاڪ واري سوني

minute hand

منٽ واري سوني

second hand

سيڪنڊن واري سوني

What time is it?

ڪيانم گهڙو ٿيو آهي؟

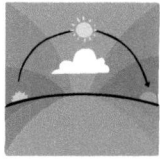

day

ڏينهن

time

وقت

now

هاڻي

digital watch

ڊجيٽل گهڙي

minute

منٽ

hour

ڪلاڪ

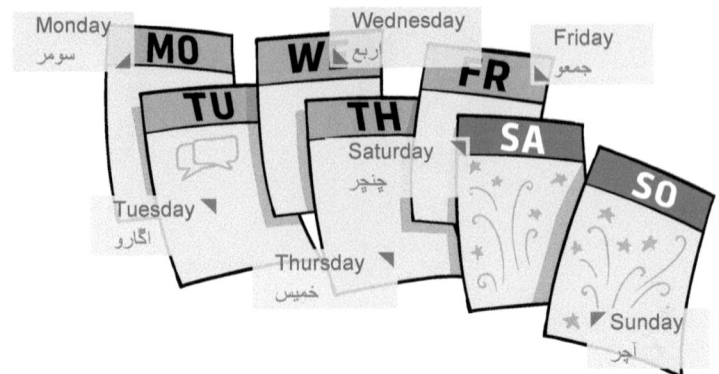

Monday
سومر

Wednesday
اربع

Friday
جمعو

Tuesday
اگارو

Saturday
ڇنڇر

Thursday
خميس

Sunday
آچر

yesterday

ڪله

today

اڄ

tomorrow

سيٺاڻي

morning

صبح

noon

منجهند

evening

شام

business days

ڪاروباري ڏينهن

weekend

هفتي جو آخر

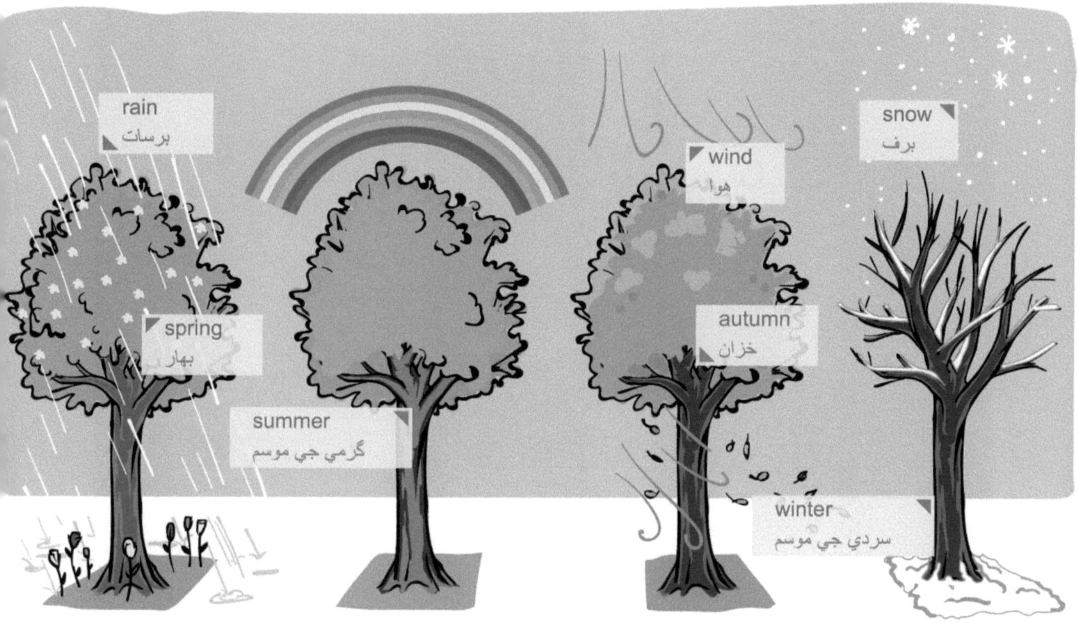

rain
برسات
spring
بهار
summer
گرمي جي موسم
wind
هوا
autumn
خزان
snow
برف
winter
سردي جي موسم

4.APRIL 11°
5.APRIL 4°
6.APRIL 13°
7.APRIL 8°
8.APRIL 10°

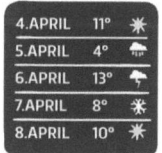

weather forecast

موسم جي پيشنگوهي

F C
120 90 60 30 0 -30
40 30 20 10 0 -10 -20

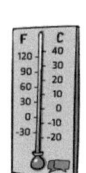

thermometer

ٿرماميٽر

sunshine

اُس

cloud

بادل

fog

ڌنڌ

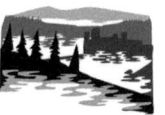

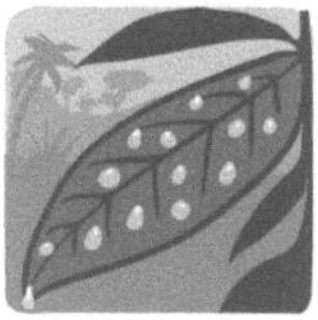

humidity

نمي

lightning

آسماني بجلي

thunder

ٹرماميٹر

storm

طوفان

hail

ڳڙ جو مينهن

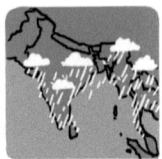

monsoon

مون سون

flood

ٻوڏ

ice

برف

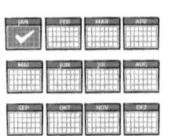

January

جنوري

February

فيبروري

March

مارچ

April

اپريل

May

مئي

June

جون

July

جولائي

August

آگسٽ

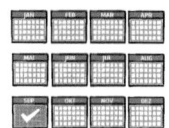

September

سيپٹمبر

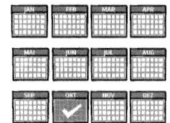

October

آکٹوبر

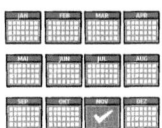

November

نومبر

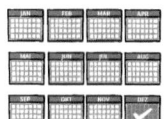

December

ڈسمبر

shapes

شکلون

circle

دائرو

square

چکور

rectangle

مستطيل

triangle

ٹکنڈي

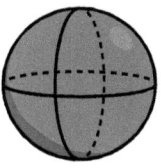

sphere

کره

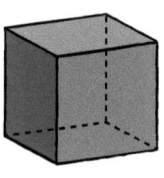

cube

کعب

white

....

اڃو

yellow

....

پيلو

orange

....

نارنجي

pink

....

گلابي

red

....

ڳاڙهو

purple

....

جامني

blue

....

نيرو

green

....

سائو

brown

....

ناسي

grey

....

پورو

black

....

ڪارو

a lot / a little

گھٹو / ٹورو

angry / calm

ناراض / پر سکون

beautiful / ugly

خوبصورت / بدصورت

beginning / end

شروعات / ختم

big / small

وڈو / نڈو

bright / dark

روشنی / اونده

brother / sister

بهن / بهاني

clean / dirty

صاف / خراب

complete / incomplete

مکمل / نا مکمل

day / night

ڈینهن / رات

dead / alive

مرده / زنده

wide / narrow

بگهو / تنگ

edible / inedible

کائڻ قابل نه هجڻ / کائڻ جي قابل هجن

evil / kind

برو / سٺو

excited / bored

پرجوش / بوريت جوشڪار

fat / thin

موٽو / پتلو

first / last

پهريون / آخري

friend / enemy

دوست / دشمن

full / empty

پريل / خالي

hard / soft

سخت / نرم

heavy / light

ڳورو / هلڪو

hunger / thirst

بک / اڃ

ill / healthy

بيمار / صحت

illegal / legal

غيرقانون / قانوني

intelligent / stupid

عقلمند / بيوقوف

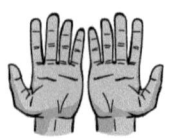

left / right

سڌو / اٻو

near / far

ويجهي / پري

new / used

ننون / استعمال ثيل

nothing / something

کجه به نه / کجه

old / young

پوڑهو / نوجوان

on / off

آن / أف

open / closed

كليل / بند

quiet / loud

خاموش / بلند آواز سان

rich / poor

امير / غريب

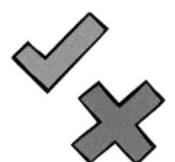

right / wrong

صحيح / غلط

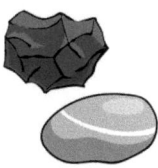

rough / smooth

کهورو / لسو

sad / happy

غمگين / خوش

short / long

مختصر / بگهو

slow / fast

آهسته / تيز

wet / dry

آلو / سكل

warm / cool

گرم / ٹھو

war / peace

جنگ / امن

0

zero

زيرو

1

one

هک

2

two

په

3

three

ڼي

4

four

چار

5

five

پنج

6

six

چه

7

seven

ست

8

eight

اٹ

9

nine

نوَ

10

ten

لّه

11

eleven

يارهن

12
twelve

بارہن

13
thirteen

تیرہن

14
fourteen

چودھن

15
fifteen

پندرہن

16
sixteen

سورہن

17
seventeen

سترہن

18
eighteen

ارڑھن

19
nineteen

اوٹویہ

20
twenty

ویہ

100
hundred

سو

1.000
thousand

ہزار

1.000.000
million

ڈہ لک

English
....
انگريزي

American English
....
آمريکي انگريزي

Chinese Mandarin
....
چيني ميندارن

Hindi
....
هندي

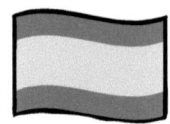

Spanish
....
اندلسي بولي

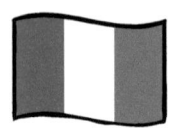

French
....
فرانسيسي

Arabic
....
عربي

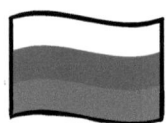

Russian
....
روسي

Portuguese
....
پرتگالي

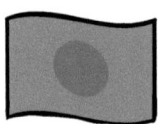

Bengali
....
بنگالي

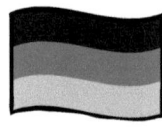

German
....
جرمن

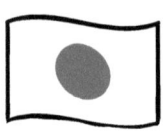

Japanese
....
جاپاني

I

مان

you

تون

he / she / it

هي چوكري/ هي چوكرو / هو

we

اسان

you

تون

they

هو

who?

كير؟

what?

چا؟

how?

كينن

where?

كٿي؟

when?

كڏهن؟

name

نالو

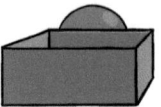

behind

پويان

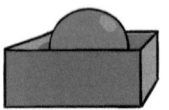

in

in front of

جي سامھون

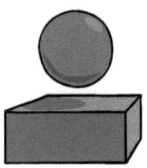

over

مٿي

on

تي

under

ھيٺ

beside

ڀرسان

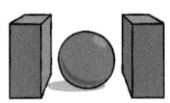

between

وچ ۾

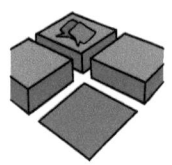

place

جڳھ